Why We Left

I Remember
BOSNIA

Anita Ganeri

RAINTREE
STECK-VAUGHN
PUBLISHERS
The Steck-Vaughn Company

Austin, Texas

Published by Raintree Steck-Vaughn Publishers, an imprint of Steck-Vaughn Company

Editors: Sally Matthews, Edith Vann
Designers: Peter Bennett, Tessa Barwick
Cover Design: Joyce Spicer
Illustrator: David Burroughs
Photo Research: Emma Krikler

Library of Congress Cataloging-in-Publication Data

Ganeri, Anita, 1961–
    I remember Bosnia / Anita Ganeri
      p. cm. — (Why we left)
    Includes index
    ISBN 0-8114-5607-2
    1. Bosnia and Herzegovina — Juvenile literature. 2. Yugoslav War, 1991- — Bosnia and Herzegovina — Juvenile literature. I. Title. II. Series
    DR1660.G36 1995
    949.7'42024–dc20   94-25548
                   CIP

Printed and bound in Belgium

1 2 3 4 5 6 7 8 9 0 PR 99 98 97 96 95 94

CONTENTS

Introduction

Hello! My name is Samira, and I am a Muslim from Bosnia. I came here just a few months ago with my family to escape from the war that is destroying my country.

Before the war, our way of life in Bosnia was like life here. We, as Muslims, were used to living in peace with Serb and Croat neighbors. But now all that has changed. Neighbor is fighting neighbor. Our towns are being ruined, in what seems like a never-ending war.

Come with me, and I'll tell you about Bosnia. I'll tell how it was before the war and what it's like now.

Bosnia declared independence from the former Yugoslavia in 1992. Since then the Serbs, Croats, and Muslims living there have been fighting. All want to seize as much land as possible. Before the war, Bosnia had a population of 4.5 million people. Three-quarters of these people have lost their homes. About 140,000 are dead or missing. Over 2 million refugees have fled to safety.

Bosnia Today

There are three main groups of people in Bosnia. They are the Serbs, the Croats, and the Muslims. Each group has its own customs and religion. There have been differences between these groups for a long time. But most people used to live and work together in peace. Now these differences have led to the bitter war between neighbors in Bosnia today.

Many different languages are spoken in Bosnia. Everyone speaks Serbo-Croatian, the official language. But many Muslims also speak Turkish or Albanian. Serbo-Croatian is written in two different alphabets. The Serbs write it in the Cyrillic alphabet, used also to write Russian. The Croats and Muslims write it in the Roman alphabet, used to write French, Spanish, and English.

zdravo
здраво

The words on the left both mean "Hello" in Serbo-Croatian. The top word is written in the Roman alphabet. The bottom word is written in the Cyrillic alphabet.

Country and Landscape

Bosnia is made up of two areas — Bosnia in the north and Herzegovina in the south. But it is usually just called Bosnia, for short. It is in an area called the Balkan Peninsula in southeastern Europe. Bosnia is a very small country, only about half the size of Kentucky. But from 1918-1992, it was part of a larger country, called Yugoslavia. At that time, Bosnia and Yugoslavia shared the same flag (right).

Bosnia's neighbors are Croatia, Serbia, and Montenegro. Along with Slovenia and Macedonia, they made up the old country of Yugoslavia. Bosnia's capital city is Sarajevo.

Bosnia has mountains but very little coastland. There are the high mountains of the Dinaric Alps. There are also flat plains, large areas of forests, and many lakes and rivers.

The Turkish bridge at Mostar (right) was one of Bosnia's most famous bridges. It was built in the sixteenth century across the Neretva River. Sadly, this beautiful, old bridge has been destroyed. It is yet another casualty of the war in Bosnia.

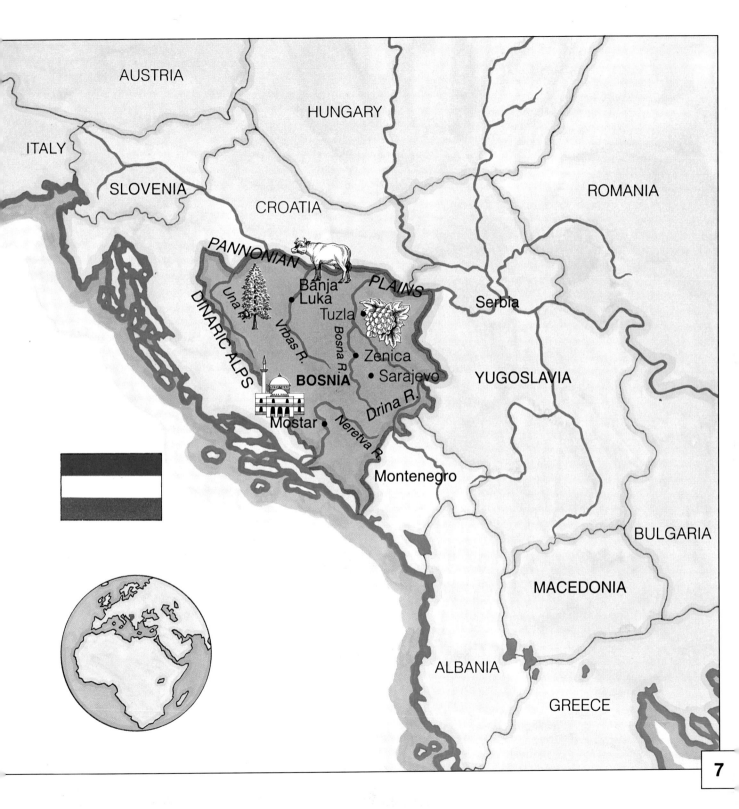

AUSTRIA

HUNGARY

ITALY

SLOVENIA

ROMANIA

CROATIA

PANNONIAN

PLAINS

Banja
Luka

Tuzla

Serbia

Una R.

Vrbas R.

Bosna R.

DINARIC ALPS

Zenica

Sarajevo

YUGOSLAVIA

BOSNIA

Drina R.

Mostar

Neretva R.

Montenegro

BULGARIA

MACEDONIA

ALBANIA

GREECE

7

Climate

Bosnia has many different kinds of weather. It also has a variety of plants and wild animals.

The winters are cold and snowy in the mountains and in the north plains. They are milder in the south. The summers are warm and rainy in the mountains. But they are dry, sunny, and very hot in the rest of the country.

Strong winds are common in Bosnia. The wind called the *jugo* brings rain. The *maestral* brings relief from the summer heat. The *bura* is a bitterly cold wind from the northeast.

The area is often struck by earthquakes. In 1979, a huge earthquake hurt many of Bosnia's towns and villages.

Fir trees cover the mountain slopes (far left). The ancient Pančić Spruce is a kind of tree. It has been on the Earth for millions of years — longer than human beings. Many wild animals live in the mountains and forests, such as wild boars, lynxes, bears, and wolves (left).

There are Muslims living all over the world. Bosnia and the rest of the former Yugoslavia is home to the biggest Muslim group in Europe (above). Most of the people who live in the Middle East, North Africa, Pakistan, and Bangladesh are Muslims. There are also large groups of Muslims in Malaysia and Indonesia. The largest group of Muslims in the world lives in India (right).

The Muslims

The first Muslims were the Arabs. In the seventh century, they began to build a huge empire. It stretched across many countries. Early in the fourteenth century, Turkish Muslims, called the Ottomans, took over Bosnia. Many Bosnians then became Muslims. Today about 40 percent of Bosnians are Muslims, like my family.

Muslim and Turkish influences remain. There are beautiful mosques, places where Muslims worship. In the cities there are colorful Turkish markets. There you can see men wearing red fez hats with flat tops and snake charmers. Children eat candy, called Turkish delight.

Some Muslim groups are very strict about how people dress. The women have to cover themselves up completely whenever they go out. This is to keep strangers from looking at them. They wear long robes and veils or masks, called *yashmaks*, like this woman from Oman (left). Most Muslim women in Bosnia have more freedom in the way they dress. But they usually cover their heads with scarves.

The Serbs and Croats

About half of the people in Bosnia are either Serbs or Croats. Their ancestors came from Poland and Russia in the sixth and seventh centuries.

The Serbs and the Croats were the two largest groups in the former Yugoslavia. Many of them lived in their own states of Serbia and Croatia. But many Serbs and Croats lived in other former Yugoslavian states, such as Bosnia.

In 1991, Croatia declared itself a separate country. The Croats had more people. They thought that the Serbs had too much power in the central Yugoslavian government. This led to a war between the Croats and the Serbs living in Croatia. This war ended in early 1992. Then the Serbs and Croats living in Bosnia started fighting over power and land. The war in Bosnia is still going on to this day.

The Serbs and Croats each have their own customs. Croatian folk dancers can be seen in villages all around Bosnia (right). Such clothes as the Croatian national dress (left) are often worn for weddings and other special occasions.

Beliefs

In the streets of Bosnia you can hear the sounds of church bells. And you can hear the chant of the *mussiens* (priests) calling Muslims to prayer. This shows the mixture of different religions.

Muslims, like me, believe in Allah (God) and the teachings of his prophet, Muhammed. He was born in the sixth century in Mecca, Saudi Arabia. We always have to face the direction of Mecca when we pray (right). The buildings where we worship are called mosques.

Most Serbs and Croats are Christians. There are many different forms of Christianity. Many Serbs belong to the Eastern Orthodox Church. Most Croats are Roman Catholics. Like other Christians, they worship in churches and cathedrals.

Different religions have different holy books. The Christians follow the teachings in the Bible. The holy book of the Muslims is the Koran (left). It contains the words that Allah passed down to Muhammed.

Our Way of Life

Our way of life in Bosnia was like that in many other developed countries. Most people lived well — better than in most other Eastern European countries. Like many other Bosnian families, my family lived in a modern apartment (right). It was just like apartments here. We also had a car and a television. My parents both had jobs. While they were at work, I went to school. My younger sister and brother went to a day-care center run by the government.

However, life in Bosnia has changed since the war began. Families have been broken up. Many homes have been harmed or torn down in the fighting.

Bosnian dishes include kebabs, spicy meat balls, and goulash stew. We also eat lots of sweet, sticky Turkish pastries, like baclava (right).

Living in the City

The capital city of Bosnia is Sarajevo (left). It is the government, business, and historical center of the country. The other major cities are Banja Luka, Zenica, Tuzla, and Mostar.

When my family and I lived in Sarajevo, it was a busy, exciting city. There was a mixture of old and new, East and West. Skyscrapers, supermarkets, and modern offices stood beside mosques and Turkish markets, called bazaars.

Today Sarajevo is a very different place. Almost every day there is fighting, and many buildings have been destroyed. Many people in the city have no electricity and very little food. They may be hit by gunfire in the streets getting the water they need to live (below right).

The currency of Bosnia is the dinar (top left). But the Bosnian economy has been ruined because of the war. Today American dollars (middle left) and German marks (bottom left) are worth more than dinars in Bosnia.

In some places, the way of farming hasn't changed for hundreds of years. People still use old-fashioned plows pulled by oxen or horses to farm their fields (above). They take their goods to market in wooden carts (right). But there are many farmers who use modern machinery and up-to-date methods of farming.

Village Life

The land in Bosnia is scattered with villages. Many village people work as farmers. They grow different kinds of crops. They raise barley, oats, oranges, lemons, grapes, plums, potatoes, and other vegetables. Many farmers also raise cattle, pigs, and sheep.

In the villages, most people live in small houses built of stone or wood. About three-quarters of village homes have electricity. Nearly all the houses have running water.

Over the past 50 years, the number of farmers in Bosnia has steadily become smaller. Before the war many farmers left their villages. They looked for better-paid jobs in the cities. Lately, many people have been forced to leave. Their villages have been destroyed in the fighting.

Bosnia has many vineyards where wine grapes are grown. Wine is a popular drink and has been made there for hundreds of years. Some Bosnian wines are sold to other countries. Two popular brands of wine are Blatina, a red wine, and Zilavka, a white wine (right).

Work and School

Before World War II, three-quarters of the people in the former Yugoslavia were farmers. After the war, the Communist government worked to change the country from a farming nation to a manufacturing country. By the 1980s, only a quarter of the people farmed. The rest worked in mining, manufacturing, building, and such businesses as restaurants and bakeries.

In Bosnia about 40 percent of the people work in industry. Bosnia's industries are making clothes and cloth, preparing food, mining coal and iron ore, making cars, and making steel.

Bosnia also has many businesspeople, teachers, lawyers, and doctors. Busiest today are the doctors and nurses looking after people wounded in the war (far right).

Bosnia also has many people with special skills. Mostar and Sarajevo are famous for their rugs and carpets. They come in many beautiful designs (right) made from brightly colored wools.

About 90 percent of people in Bosnia can read and write. Education is free. All children from the age of 7 to 14 go to school. When I lived in Sarajevo, I went to a special Muslim school (below). Unlike my school here, the boys and girls were separated into different classes. Like here, we studied many different subjects. But we also had to spend time every day learning about Islam and reading the Koran.

Soccer is very popular in Bosnia. The former Yugoslavia had a world-class soccer team (right). It reached the quarter finals of the World Cup in 1990. Children also love to play soccer. It doesn't matter if there is no official soccer field. They can always make their own goal out of old plastic bags, netting, and string (above).

Sports and Leisure

Just like children in other countries, we like to watch television and listen to pop music. We read comics, play games, and go to the movies after school or on weekends.

The mountains provide different sporting activities as well. Hunting and hiking are both popular. There are high peaks for people who enjoy mountain climbing. In the winter many people go skiing. In the summer they enjoy swimming and fishing in the lakes.

In the evening many people take part in an old practice called *korzo*. They walk along the main street of their town. And they stop to chat with the friends they meet. They may also go to one of the many coffeehouses, which are called *kafanas*.

Bosnia is proud of its world-famous ski slopes. Many people believe that the snow on Mount Bjelasnica, near Sarajevo, is the deepest and best in Europe. In 1984, Sarajevo hosted the Winter Olympic Games. The Olympic mascot was a fox called Vucko (left). Vucko could be seen everywhere in the city — on posters, in the stores, and on the television. His face became known all over the world.

Why I'm Here

Bosnia declared itself independent in 1992. Since then it has become a battlefield for a war among the Serbs, Croats, and Muslims.

The quarreling groups are fighting each other over land. Thousands of people on all sides are being wounded and killed. One of the terrible parts of this war is "ethnic cleansing." This happens when one group of people tries to force all other different groups from the land. They want to drive them from homes where their families have lived for many, many years (right).

Despite peace talks, the war continues. This is why my family came to this country. It was just too dangerous for us to stay in Bosnia any longer.

From 1943–1980, the Communist leader Josip Broz Tito (right) united the different states and ethnic groups of Yugoslavia. But after his death in 1980, old quarrels began again. The Communist Party lost control, and Yugoslavia was split into separate countries.

The Future

I don't know what will happen to my country. So many places have been destroyed. So many people have lost their homes. It will take years for the thousands who fled to return to Bosnia and have a peaceful life. Whatever happens, it will never be the same again. The country may be divided among the Serbs, Croats, and Muslims. Now the only thing people have to look forward to are the food and supplies brought by the United Nations trucks (left). Sometimes, even these are stopped by the fighting.

I have been in this country for only a few months now. And it still feels very strange. But I have started going to school and am learning to speak the language. Over here I can live peacefully. I have friends and neighbors of all different races and religions. I still have nightmares about the gunfire in Sarajevo. But I know that I am one of the lucky ones. I am safe in my new home.

Fact File

Land and People

Official name: Republic of Bosnia and Herzegovina

Main language: Serbo-Croatian

Other languages: Turkish, Albanian

Population: 4.5 million (prewar population)

Cities

Capital city: Sarajevo

Other major cities: Banja Luka, Zenica, Tuzla, Mostar

Weather

Climate: Cold winters and hot summers

Landmarks

Major rivers: Neretva, Bosna, Drina, Una, Vrbas

Highest mountain: Maglic 7,828 ft. (2,386 m) above sea level

Culture

Main religions: Islam, Roman Catholic, Eastern Orthodox

Ethnic groups: Bosnian Muslim (40%), Serb (32%), Croat (18%)

Literacy rate: 90 percent

Government

Form of government: Multi-party Republic (at present)

Head of state: President

Eligibility to vote: Universal (at present)

Food and Farming

Crops: Corn, barley, oats, wheat, potatoes, plums, grapes, citrus fruits

Trade and Industry

Mineral resources: Iron ore, coal, lignite, bauxite, rock salt, asbestos

Industries: Iron and steel works, chemicals, car and machinery manufacture, metal and lumber products, mining, food processing, clothing, and textiles

Major exports: Machinery, high quality clothing and footwear, chemicals

Major imports: Raw materials, petroleum-based fuels, consumer goods

Currency: Dinar

Index

Photographic Credits:
Front cover: Panos Pictures; Front cover inset, pp. 3, 29: Roger Vlitos; Title page, pp. 10 (bottom), 11, 15, 17, 18, 23 (both), 24 (both), 25, 27, 28: Frank Spooner Pictures; pp. 4, 6, 9, 12, 13, 19, 20 (both): Eye Ubiquitous; p. 10 (top): Spectrum Colour Library.